MID LIFE
CELEBRATION

rethink · reprioritize · recommit

jeff noel

Sooner or later it becomes crystal clear. Life is not a dress rehearsal. So I am here to remind you why today is not a good day to put your dreams on hold.

Midlife crisis is spending our life chasing our dreams and finally getting there, more or less. But in looking around, we think, this is not what I wanted.

DEDICATION

Bless us, O Lord, and these Thy gifts
which we are about to receive, from Thy bounty,
through Christ our Lord. Amen.

We pray for peace in our soul, joy in our spirit,
and love in our heart, for all our family, all our friends,
and especially all those people less fortunate.

PROLOGUE

The two most magnificent days in our lives are the day we are born and the day we figure out why.

The day we were born. No brainer.

The day we figure out why. Epic revelation.

If you are like me, you spent your life working hard to go after and achieve your dreams. Those lofty, noble and grand dreams we dreamt as young adults. Remember?

And in the process we finally arrive at the place we dreamt of, look around and say, this isn't what I wanted!

Some call it a midlife crisis while others call it a wake up call. No matter the name, the result is the same and a game-changing question must be asked.

Now what?

This is a story about our journey as human beings to find peace and contentment in a world that attacks the very essence of these two vital, but simple ideals.

It's a true story.

And a story that will help you **rethink** your life, help **reprioritize** your life and offer hope in your ability to **recommit** your life to a new set of priorities.

Never allow your memories to be bigger than your dreams.

Ready? Let's go.

TABLE OF CONTENTS

THE BEGINNING
(HOW WE GOT HERE)

THERE IS A QUIET MOVEMENT UNDERWAY

The movement is called authenticity.
We cherish it in others.

We long for it ourselves.

But humans are afraid. I am afraid. You are afraid. So we all put up a good front. You should never allow yourself to appear vulnerable or appear weak, right? Not a good career move.

So we become someone we are not. Unintentionally. And this becomes a habit. And this habit, over time, becomes what we think and do, without thinking.

What we think and do, without thinking.

Going through the motions.

We pollute our soul so slowly we never notice. We become the person we set out to become. We are, after all, clever, dedicated and persistent.

As we progress in our careers, we can hear the echoes of that great motto, carpe diem.

Seize the day, right? Do not waste career opportunities. Live life to the fullest. Be somebody. Be successful. Climb that ladder. How can we not?

Eventually and predictably though, something very bad happens. We become robots on the treadmill of life. Pausing to reflect was easy in our youth. We had the time. We lacked the pressure of adult responsibility.

But pause and reflect now? Seriously? Who has got time? Maybe later we will have time, but not now.

But now is here, today, and in our quest for prosperity and happiness, we have become slaves to our bank accounts. Our work is our mistress. We worry about what others will think of us. Everything else takes a back seat.

And so it goes, another day, another dollar.

THE NATURE OF
LIFE IS CHANGE

The more things change the more they stay the same. The only constant is change. Sayings about change are a dime a dozen. We carry around a nickel's worth.

Carpe Diem, seize the day. Whatever, right? It no longer triggers inspiration. It simply pours out of our mouth or into our thoughts like going to the bathroom when we first awake.

No thought whatsoever. Habit. Routine. Walking zombie.

We must change this. We can change this. Often in life, the most profound change begins with the smallest tweak.

What if carpe diem was not a motto or cliché as society has coined it?

What if carpe diem became an honest to goodness battle cry!

Carpe diem: Live, before you die!

So there is the small tweak...

Live, before you die.

Yes.

Got it?

Live.

Before you die.

If the nature of life is change, and change can grow from the tiniest of seeds, here are three small seeds for you to begin to discover your **second** magnificent day:

Rethink, reprioritize, and recommit.

Rethink. Everything.

Reprioritize. Reshuffle our priorities.

Recommit. Move forward with renewed conviction.

Life is hard for everyone, leaving us with only two painfully real choices:

1. Give up
2. Don't give up

The nature of life is change.

We know this.

THERE ARE TWO KINDS OF PEOPLE

Some people make things happen and others let things happen. It is what it is. We know this too.

Those who respond to change are simply surviving.

Those who anticipate change thrive.

Respond or anticipate.

React or plan.

Big difference. You know this.

The big question is which one are you?

And the second big question is are you satisfied?

And the final question is do you care about any of this?

If you have a deep, profound desire to be more satisfied, than your answer is self-explanatory.

Our answer tells us we have a magnificent opportunity and readjustment ahead of us.

This of course will take time.

EACH DAY THE ONLY THING WE ALL GET IN EQUAL AMOUNTS IS TIME

If there is one great equalizer in the world, it's time. Served up in equal portions to every living being — 24 hours each day. It's also unerringly predictable.

The sun will rise tomorrow. Guaranteed.

What if we believed the workday begins the night before? And each morning we were to hit the ground running with the glorious gift of the next 24 hours?

To not do this is to be unprepared to face the day ahead and can be called surviving.

To prepare before the day begins and to know the day's priorities can be called thriving.

This does not have to feel elusive.

In fact, it should not be elusive.

You are in charge. Be prepared.

There can be no excuse from anyone that time is unfair, that some get more. No one gets more. You know this.

WHAT WAS TRUE FOR YOU AS A CHILD MAY NOT BE TRUE FOR YOU AS AN ADULT

Sure, there is joyful, uninhibited thinking and doing as a child. We ran around naked, screaming, laughing, grabbing, and playing. We could not be embarrassed back then. No one in diapers, even smelly ones, can ever be embarrassed.

Walk around in smelly pants now and what would happen?

As youth we were free to make mistakes. Look how long it took us to walk or to go number two in the potty. It took even longer to understand that we should clean our face after eating a melting ice cream cone.

Who cares what we look like? That thought never crossed our mind. Well, not until junior high school.

So yeah, what was true for us as a child is no longer true for us as an adult.

YOU WILL EVENTUALLY DIE — HOW YOU LIVE BETWEEN NOW AND THEN IS UP TO YOU

When I randomly ask people, what is the meaning of life they pause with a blank, confused or guilty stare, and say that is a great question.

Sure it is a great question. In fact it is the most important question you will ever be asked.

So be ready and let your answer roll off your tongue with the ease and quickness of other simple questions like, what is two + two?

The point is not to have a correct answer for the meaning of life, but rather, simply to have one that you believe in — with all your heart, your entire mind and all your strength.

Can you picture yourself in a place where it rolls off your tongue?

When you can do that, how you decide to live will come more naturally. Not easily, because everyone fights a hard battle, but easier.

JEFF'S CLOCK AND PURPOSE

I was born June 8, 1959, but did not figure out why until 40 years later. Plus, it has taken an additional 14 years to get this book in your hands. If you are already certain why you are here on our planet, well, you are not reading this.

Since you *are* reading this, you have a gut feeling that this book will help you think, smile and be grateful as you discover your second most magnificent day.

There is great truth in clichés. Take this cliché for instance, better late than never.

I discovered, nearing age 50, that when our young son started looking for the face of Jesus in the real world, I did not want him to have to look any further than across the dinner table.

When this revelation — this epiphany — hit me, it changed everything.

Better late than never.

The way I lived my life up to that point was entirely internally focused.

Sound familiar?

When I realized that a young person would be watching my every move, it hit me:

It matters little to walk to do life's preaching; if not our walking **is** the preaching.

11

This book's key message is that you must take personal responsibility to be a great role model for the people you love.

If you don't, this book, and your efforts, will waste your time.

A KICK IN THE BACKSIDE

Our son's pre-K teacher called it tough love. And it is. Observe the laws of nature when a mother bear is raising her cubs; if they do something that almost gets them killed, mother bear lashes out at them.

Get between a mother bear and her cub and you are in big trouble. There is a primal, parental instinct — first to protect and then to instruct — all done for the end goal, which is for the survival and the propagation of the species.

This book is **intended to inspire you to start** taking transformational action and to inspire you to go from surviving to thriving.

This book is **also intended** to encourage you to stop going through the motions and consider going for the gold, and from wandering aimlessly to being crystal clear, and from being a warning to being the example.

WHAT IS MIDLIFE?

Midlife is relative. Throw out the stereotypes of the middle aged, receding hairline, pot-bellied executive who buys the red convertible sports car and chases after younger women.

Trash that stereotype. That is not what this is about.

My senior year in high school a good friend and teammate, Jim Silcox, died in a tragic car accident. When was his midlife?

My sister's precious first child lived 10 days. When was Jack's midlife?

Midlife can happen at any time, in many ways.

For the sake of this story, I am defining midlife as a stage in life between young adulthood and old age.

Again, the actual age of a person when midlife starts can vary. The assumption here, however, is that we have been through many of life's ups and downs and have had copious opportunities to change, but we did not.

OUR SOCIETY HAS BEEN INADEQUATE AT PREPARING US FOR MIDLIFE

How many of us were taught massive lessons on personal responsibility while in elementary school learning to read, write, add and subtract?

Most likely the answer is none.

What we were generally taught in school was how to stay out of trouble (conform) while we were there.

Conformity. We were taught nothing of the big picture in life. Not really.

No one insisted and reinforced that failure to exercise regularly or eat a balanced diet would catch up with us in a way that could leave us feeling hopeless.

No one emphatically stressed the critical difference in our choice of friends, the language we used, what we read, watched, and listened to — no one warned us we are a product of our environment and all our choices contribute to our attitude's landscape.

No one unquestionably convinced us that love is all that matters. Public education did not teach us we are here to love and be loved, to serve others, and not be served.

This allowed us to grow up selfishly thinking we were the center of the universe.

On top of that no one encouraged us to think about a career doing something we would love. And how enjoying our career would facilitate thriving.

Rather, get a good job to pay the bills, put food on the table and a roof over our head.

Surviving.

Just like in nature every ant in the ant colony makes a contribution. So does every bee in the beehive.

And it is the same with humans except society pays humans with money.

And more money is not necessarily better.

And no one taught us the administrative duties required for running the business of our existence — the paperwork of life. That most of life's challenges are created (and resolved) in proportion to our personal organization.

The absence of formal preparation for personal responsibility continues all the way through the first six stages of life: from our birth through young adulthood.

A HARSH REALITY

And then one day without warning, we come face to face with a harsh reality.

We have outgrown young adulthood and have entered into maturity: life's final three stages.

What triggers our acute awareness unlike never before are common midlife moments.

But before we see some typical midlife moments, let us review life's nine grand stages.

GROWING UP:
LIFE'S FIRST (SIX) STAGES

1. Birth
2. Infancy
3. Childhood
4. Puberty
5. Adolescence
6. Young Adulthood

MATURITY: LIFE'S FINAL (THREE) STAGES

1. Midlife
2. Old Age
3. Death

MIDLIFE MOMENTS

We may experience one or more of these:

Declining health

Grandchildren

Retirement

Inheritance

Becoming outdated

No longer being the most important person in anyone's life

Gaining wisdom

Passing the torch

Death

Tragedy

Divorce

Marriage

Bankruptcy

THE ASTONISHING TRUTH ABOUT OUR PLACE IN LIFE

There is no going back. No do over.

And there is no jumping ahead. No skipping our turn.

We are undeniably where we are – mentally, physically, spiritually, at work, and at home.

We are responsible for all of it.

And we are responsible for thriving or surviving.

This is truth.

No one else is responsible for where we are right now.

No one.

And we know this.

OUR CULTURE'S RELATIONSHIP WITH YOUTH AND AGING

Society didn't set out to be cruel, yet everywhere we turn salt is being thrown on our midlife wounds.

Our self-esteem unfortunately, if linked to external attributes such as appearance, status, title, and other external indicators slowly erodes over time.

Everywhere we look youth sells and this is poison.

Our self-esteem can only be salvaged if we are beautiful on the inside, and if our overall wellness feels balanced.

Balance is incredibly elusive.

And when chased after, difficult to catch and grab hold of.

Why? Because everyone we know is trying to survive.

The notion of thriving and having balance is pushed aside for when we have more time and energy.

We think this will happen when we retire.

And there is a decent chance it may never happen. This book is designed to help you see that.

RETHINK

OUR MIDLIFE CRISIS HAPPENED BECAUSE WE INVESTED OUR SECURITY IN THINGS THAT CHANGE

The biggest mistake we can make is when we believe we have figured everything out and then settle into a routine, only to wake up one day painfully aware that we missed the boat.

The antidote is to anticipate change, not adapt or react to it.

We know this.

Yet we wait.

And do nothing.

And the waiting becomes an insidious habit.

As does doing nothing.

The twin siblings of self-destruction are waiting and doing nothing.

Habits.

Unbreakable habits.

BRIDGING THE GAP BETWEEN HABITS AND TRUTHFUL AWARENESS

Habits are what we think and do, without thinking. Habits are developed early.

Habits define who we are.

Habits are good and bad.

Habits are hard to change.

Habits are not invincible.

Habits can be conquered.

It will be infinitely easier to quit than try to change.

Right? Take the path of least resistance.

At least that is the quickest conclusion most of us make. And it is deadly.

We can change. We must change.

How can we not?

Is quitting our journey to thrive what we want our loved ones to see, feel, and model?

AWARENESS VERSUS IGNORANCE

This one is real simple. Ignoring basic life facts doesn't change them or make them go away. Ignoring the facts also doesn't skew them in our favor.

Not paying careful attention to everything that influences our attitude will make us less positive than someone who does.

Not exercising regularly, not resting adequately and not eating appropriately is going to make us less healthy than someone who does.

Not praying, helping, serving, or volunteering is going to make our spirit less resilient to life's challenges and less receptive to life's joys, than someone who does.

Not reading, not taking classes, not studying, and not teaching others is going to make us less educated, and paid less, than someone who does.

Not developing, creating, experimenting and polishing our organizational skills will leave us feeling more overwhelmed and helpless than someone who does.

RESPONSIBILITY VERSUS BALANCE

Balance is an equal devotion to life's biggest choices. Our lifelong, balanced devotion is a huge personal responsibility.

This is profoundly simple and simply profound.

Life has five big choices.

Mind, body, spirit, money and hq.

Mind, body and spirit are self-explanatory.

Money is about our work life.

HQ is our headquarters or home life.

Being personally responsible is key to finding peace and contentment.

Doing what needs to be done, when it needs to be done, whether we like it or not.

No peace without balance. No contentment without peace.

The beauty in living with peace and contentment is that we become an example for others, rather than an unhappy and regretful warning.

SECRETS AND LIES

The secret is, there are no secrets. We know this.

And lies are everywhere. Constantly. We know this too.

And it's also no secret that most people lie to themselves, because that's how many humans cope. And it's criminal.

There is time-tested wisdom that needs no explanation. The truth hurts. And the truth can set us free. We know this. But do we embrace it?

How do we find a different, better, and more effective way to cope with this empowering wisdom? The best place to start is to **rethink** our dreams. This will take time and motivation.

If we lack time, motivation, or both, we will become frustrated. This is why a wake up call works to our advantage. Our wake up call compels us to put up or shut up.

The gift of our pain and discouragement, that is overwhelming at times, is our huge opportunity to take personal responsibility to fix it.

But there is a catch. The catch is we have to rearrange our priorities.

RETHINK

To rethink means to *seriously* engage in conscious examination of our priorities and direction in life.

This is almost exclusively prompted by some major life wake up call — we are forced to question everything we believe in — basically, the way in which we have led our lives.

Not only is the wake up call painful, but so is the reflection immediately afterwards.

This is the best thing that can ever happen to us.

Pause.

Yes.

Is it truly the best thing to ever happen to us?

Why?

Because bad things we cannot control will always happen.

No one is immune and we know this.

This goes back to the belief that planning allows people to thrive and reacting causes people to merely survive.

The solution to moving past merely surviving is to use our personal responsibility to live in an intentional way so that when bad things happen, our lives have already been lived without regret.

Regret is the silent, lingering enemy that attacks our peace and contentment.

Being intentional means taking control of what is

controllable.

Being intentional means life is not a spectator sport.

Being intentional means moving from the passenger seat to the driver's seat.

And being in the driver's seat now gets us ever closer to discovering our second most magnificent day.

How cool is that?

Remember when we were learning to drive we were taught to be sure to always adjust our side view and rear view mirrors?

Why? To see the bigger picture all around us and not just what is ahead of us.

HOW DID I GET HERE?

The first question we ask is an obvious question, how did I get here?

Looking back in our rear view mirror, we got here one day at a time. Quietly. Unintentionally. Ignorantly.

But now we are in the driver's seat. And the reality is we rarely look in the rearview mirror of life.

Luckily for us, we are now more keenly aware and in these glorious new moments we realize life is not a dress rehearsal.

And if this life is not a practice round and we are now crystal clear about this, what do we need to do next?

It is fundamental. Begin to uncover who you really are.

Who is the real you?

Who is your authentic self?

Who is the person you are deep down inside?

You know, the person not swayed by conformity or fitting into some prescribed mold.

WHO AM I?
(WHO DO I WANT TO BE?)

Assuming we have the courage to look, this is the first time in years, maybe decades, in which we start paying attention to what we see in the mirror.

Pausing, we now have the courage to look, painful as it might be, and face the mirror.

And we realize the youthful, ambitious dreamer we used to be has aged. A lot.

This is not the end of the world. It is a real, honest to goodness second chance.

And we are taking it because we now fully understand it was not our fault that we lived with inadequate knowledge and training about our obligation for personal responsibility.

We are also aware if we do not embrace our glorious second chance, it will be our fault and no one else's.

Times flies. When we are having fun and even when we are not.

The good news is we have an opportunity ahead of us that is the biggest one ever.

THE YOUTHFUL EXPECTATIONS OF ADULTHOOD

When we were younger, we would look at older people and swear we would be so much smarter.

They acted old and looked old.

A perfect example of what not to do or be, we thought.

We also figured they made mistakes we would never make.

Guess again.

The exuberance of our youth and our undeniable blue sky, no limits dreaming never prepared us for adult responsibility.

In spite of this, we still managed to chase and catch a few of our crazy, youthful dreams.

Lucky us.

God is good like that.

THE BIKE TRIP (1982)

I observed many people living with regrets for things they wished they'd done when they were younger.

Having premonitions is common among youth.

Acting on them, not so much.

But what if acting on premonitions became a priority?

Riding a bicycle across the country was firmly planted on my bucket list of things to do before I got a real job and a career. I was only 14 when this happened, crossing the Colorado Rockies on a Boy Scout cross-country bus trip.

As our bus chugged slowly and comfortably up the mountain pass, we passed three bicyclists enjoying the stunning vista as well as the smells, the sounds, the wind, and the sun. I imagined them taking as long as they wanted, whenever they wanted, to enjoy their trip.

Sure, most bucket lists are things to do *before* we die.

But the thought of dying never crossed my mind. The thought of living with regret deeply motivated me, even at the tender age of 14.

THERE WAS A TIME
YOU ACTED WITHOUT FEAR

Can you recall a time when this was true for you?

Nine years after that cross-country bus ride, I didn't know it at the time, but I was living without the fear of death. It was glorious. There also was very little regret.

Here is how it played out at the age of 23.

Leaving Philadelphia with $75 cash, no tent, a small cook stove, on an 18-speed touring bicycle, heading to Washington State was exciting. I knew I would run out of money eventually. And I would worry about it then.

I was certain this exciting journey, by design, would teach some great life lessons that a classroom could never teach.

I knew if I did not do this before I settled down, got a real job, married, and made monthly mortgage payments, there would never be another opportunity.

This is how the bucket list concept got started. But creating a bucket list is like phony insurance. The mere fact of having a bucket list convinces us we will have time to accomplish all our lofty to-dos.

Midlife wake up calls shatter that illusion.

FEAR IS LEARNED

I believe we don't fear death as much as we fear dying before we have really, truly lived.

We are taught to put things off.

Put things off so we can have fun now.

Put something off because we are afraid to do it now but hope later we won't be.

Put things off so we can focus on becoming successful.

Most of this is self-taught, learned behavior as we observe the adults ahead of us.

Ironically what we really fear most though is the proverbial notion of sucking the marrow out of life: actively living each day to the fullest extent possible.

You know, this ideal that when we come to die we do not have the painful realization we had not yet begun to really live.

In reality it takes guts to suck the marrow out of life.

And having the courage to be bold and daring amongst the herd is uncomfortable and scary.

SLEEPWALKING THROUGH LIFE

I have never sleepwalked and have never seen another person do it either.

As far as anyone can tell, sleepwalking is difficult to stop and potentially very dangerous.

But in reality we are all sleepwalking through life.

The metaphorical equivalent to this is called the rat race.

The rat race is also known as living on autopilot or going through the motions like everyone else in the herd.

ENTERTAINED, MEDICATED, AND DISTRACTED

The rat race is hard. And crowded. Keeping up with the Joneses. Making more money and then buying bigger, better things. Never getting ahead.

Always just getting by.

Keeping up is difficult and no one talks openly about it. We all secretly do what everyone else is doing even if it causes us anxiety from the strain.

More. Better. Faster.

From a distance it looks like a party, living life to the fullest, right?

Closer inspection reveals the truth. We are all entertained, medicated, and distracted.

Seriously.

Ouch.

This should not be a surprise to anyone.

DO WE RECOGNIZE OUR WAKEUP CALL?

Somewhere during life's party, the phone rings and on the other end we hear, hello may I speak with the owner of your life?

At first we think it is a wrong number and hang up.

But the phone rings again and again. We ignore these calls and let them go to voice mail and later hit delete.

While deleting our messages makes us feel we have handled the situation, we have in fact only made a potentially bad situation worse.

EXAMPLES OF
WAKEUP CALLS

E ventually however, the tone of the call changes.
There is an undeniable realization that there is bad news and it is critical that we pay attention.

Poor health.

Serious illness.

Disease.

Crumbled relationship.

Job loss.

Death.

Tragedy.

ASLEEP. AWAKE.

Without realizing it, we have been asleep while cruising on autopilot.

How?

Because we have been entertained, medicated, and distracted. Remember?

While the wake up call is exceptionally uncomfortable and may even be devastating news, it can also be the best thing that has ever happened to us.

This is a really important moment.

We have one of two options.

We can be devastated or we can be motivated.

We get to pick one.

This takes us back to **rethinking**.

SEE WHERE YOU ARE HEADING IS TAKING YOU?

Hitting the proverbial snooze button on life and downplaying the severity is a sure sign of our denial.

Denial is a common prescription for avoiding hard choices and hard work.

It is the herd's natural reaction to deny the truth and to look for excuses, or medication, or distractions, or entertainment to mask the pain.

All this does is make the debt collector more determined to get your undivided attention on the next call.

Ignoring what is ahead of you does not make it go away.

It surely does not and you know this.

And knowing this is a huge opportunity for you.

And your opportunity is a simple one.

It is finally your chance to break away from the herd.

LOST — FOLLOWING THE HERD

The herd mentality is an interesting phenomenon and an integral part of modern society. The primal pack. There is strength in numbers. It is a simple law of survival.

But enter the 21st century with the automobile and the light bulb.

Then there were these little things called the industrial revolution and television and the atomic bomb.

The Internet.

The iPhone.

If everyone is using it, doing it, or needs it, well then, it must be right.

And so we learn to follow the herd and we appreciate the strength and security in belonging to (and conforming with) the herd.

There is a strong feeling of security to be among the masses.

But what if the masses have it wrong?

SOMETIMES THE HERD IS LOST

When we mismanage our priorities, and nearly everyone does at some point in life, we are headed toward confrontation. This is a law that is nearly as absolute as gravity.

Okay, so the herd is entertained, medicated, and distracted.

If the herd does not care about consequences, why should I?

The herd knows best. Right?

Look at the herd mentality statistics for divorce, obesity, addiction, and financial unpreparedness. How is any of this acceptable?

Much like (the stereotypical) lemmings.

(By the way, lemmings do not commit mass suicide. That is folklore. But you get the picture.)

COMPLICITY — IT IS OKAY TO...

It is okay to do things if everyone else is doing them, right? Throw caution to the wind and common sense out the door.

Why? Because the entire herd is heading to a party.

We do not want to be late. Everywhere you look, there is a party.

Indulge, medicate, have fun, live a little. Everyone else is.

That is a sure sign it is okay.

Our friends would not steer us wrong, right?

Our neighbors, the people we live next to for part or all our life, they would not mislead us, right?

NEIGHBORS

Unless you have massive amounts of acreage, you are bound to have many neighbors. Some you will never know and others just might become your party buddies.

There is nothing wrong with drinking a beer (or three) to wash away the day's troubles.

Ah, the daily grind, the daily stress, the worries of tomorrow, the regrets of yesterday.

Nothing a few drinks cannot remedy, at least for today.

And since we are all adults we can do whatever we want.

THE HERD DOES NOT KNOW NOR CARE WHAT IS IN YOUR BEST INTEREST

The herd is the herd. No one will single you out, recognizing how special, unique, and needy you are.

No one.

And yet we place all our trust in the herd.

Why?

How?

THE HERD SEEKS COMFORT AND STATUS

If everyone is doing it that makes it okay.

Everyone would not be doing it if it were not okay. Right?

And if it is okay, that means I do not have to think, worry, or address my real issues.

Who needs another drink?

THE HERD IS INSECURE

The herd is insecure and always has been. There's strength in numbers. As long as we are not too young, too slow, too old or injured, we can stay near the center of the herd — making it hard for the outside world to find us.

In nature the predators seek the easiest kill. And the most reliable place to find that is on the edges.

Out of fear we stay in the middle with the rest of our insecure buddies.

We can all live happily ever after in the land of denial.

LOOK FOR THE MEANINGFUL REASONS

Eventually, by the blessing of our wake up call(s), we begin to wonder if there is a better herd.

We rethink our priorities, analyzing the pros and cons of following our current herd's path.

We begin to daydream again like we did as children, about how life might be more meaningful, more rewarding, more creative.

How our unique skill or gift could be used for the greater good of a different herd.

The old party is over. And a new party is being organized.

And our new party has a multitude of unexplored opportunities.

This is scary.

And exciting.

But it is mostly scary.

Which deep down is the reason we avoided the new party to begin with.

Well, that and the fact no one ever invited us before.

THE ROAD TO PARENTHOOD

With infinite ignorance, I admit I thought parenting was an entitlement. For some it is anything but. My wife and I found out the hard way.

For many reasons, there are people who will never become parents. This is either due to a law of nature, a personal choice, or a complete mystery.

The natural law is that we are put here to reproduce. Without reproduction there is no herd. Nor is there life. It would all end. Basic law.

As a 40-something career-aspiring professional, the realization that I was born to be a father and most likely was not going to be one shook my world.

Hard.

Bring you to your knees hard.

Wake up call hard.

REPRIORITIZE

JUST GO TO THE LIBRARY AND GET SOME BOOKS

After eight years, which included five on our own and three with varying degrees of insurance coverage, Cheryl becomes pregnant.

I asked Cheryl, Do you know how to be a Mom? No, she replied. Do you know how to be a Dad, she asked back. The same sorry reply as hers, no.

No worries honey, I will just go to the library and get some books.

There are a gazillion parenting books. They cannot all be saying something different. So where should I start?

Ironically there is also no manual for breaking away from the herd. So where should we start?

Because there is no clear path, I set out to distill the volumes of parenting advice down to the key, foundational basics. During this process I discovered life's five big choices.

Fortunately, the same five choices used for raising a child can be used to live and thrive with personal responsibility.

In fact, it is exactly how I run my own life.

MONTY RAY AND THE WISE OLD WOMAN

For so long the dream to become parents seemed impossible and the mountain of hope at the beginning of the journey eroded to a molehill.

You experience one unforeseen setback after another. You endure one gut wrenching heartbreak after another. Your life savings disappear.

And then something magical happens stemming from of all things, what some might call a heavenly miracle.

Feeling overwhelmed is common when faced with the realization that your biggest dream is finally going to come true.

Then enter one random, casual conversation.

You can know someone for years and never have a meaningful conversation until one day...

I hear you're going to finally become a Father, Monty Ray said as I walked through his warehouse.

Yeah, got any advice, I chimed.

Monty Ray proceeded to share a story about the day his son was born:

Jeff, I was admiring my newborn son through the nursery window when I see someone coming down the long hospital hallway. Finally, I realized it was a wise old woman, maybe

95 years old. I had this stereotype that she was going to ask if one of the newborns was mine and I would say yes and then she would go off on a long lecture about what I should do and when I should do it. I really didn't have the physical or emotional energy for that.

And sure enough, Jeff, she asked the question I predicted and of course I said yes. Next she said, everyone is going to try to tell you how to raise your child. What to do and what not to do. They will tell you when to do it and when not to.

Monty Ray continued sharing the woman's conversation by asking me, you know what happened next? She said, you only need to remember two things, just two things. You can't hold them too much and you can't love them too much.

Suddenly equipped with the big picture, I never went to the library to get any books.

And the expected birth of our Son was only a few months away.

DON'T TAKE THE GIRL

To live without our music would seem impossible to do, for in this world of troubles, our music can pull us through. The reason iPods and iTunes are off the chart successful is because music soothes the savage beast.

Songs cement special moments in time, usually milestones in our life. Hearing one of those special songs again can transport us back there in an instant.

And there are songs that we hear over and over again before we hear them for the first time. Country music's Tim McGraw released *Don't Take The Girl* in 1994. It is a song I had heard a dozen times before finally listening to the lyrics for the first time on that afternoon bicycle ride.

The song's main character is a little boy who doesn't want his dad to bring along a little girl on their father and son fishing trip.

So he says to his father, Dad, don't take the girl.

The song ends with the little boy and little girl now grown, married, and at the hospital for the birth of their first child. But life-threatening complications are occurring in the delivery room.

There I was, a grown man, listening to the radio, crying as I rode my bicycle home.

A few years later, just hours before our son was born, I

envisioned myself as the lead character. Cheryl had been in labor for over 24 hours. The baby's head was bent (stuck) and multiple attempts using a suction device were unsuccessful.

The baby's heart was racing at 180-190 beats per minute, for what seemed like forever.

Finally, Cheryl was quickly moved to an operating room for an emergency caesarian delivery.

There I was deliriously sitting in the hall outside the operating room.

Something felt drastically wrong. Everything was taking far too long and no one was telling me anything.

This could not be good. And I pictured the worst-case scenario.

I figured a child would need his mother more than his father in those early years, so on bended knee I prayed to God, *don't take the girl*, but if you feel you must, would you please take me instead.

The herd was becoming less and less important.

REPRIORITIZE

If **rethink** is defined: *To seriously engage in conscious examination of our priorities and direction in life,* then **reprioritize** means exactly that: We shuffle the deck for our life's priorities into a different order. We may add new priorities that had been dormant or missing. We might also eliminate old, long-standing and less important priorities. In short, we **reprioritize**.

Bottom line? There is a new sheriff in town.

LIFE IS NOT FAIR: JEFF AND DAD

Life is not fair. Get used to it. We have heard this since we were old enough to start caring whether there was melted ice cream dried on our face.

Your Dad is retiring early.

Why? I asked.

He can no longer perform his job well enough.

So Dad quickly retires with early onset, rapid progression Alzheimer's disease. No one ever saw that one coming.

Growing up Dad and I rarely talked. I do not recall any special fatherly advice that has stuck with me. No sayings, no traditions, no wise tidbits. He was a busy man working three jobs. He was a great provider.

After Dad passed away my family reassured me Dad loved me very much. I believed it, and still do. He and I missed the opportunity for more time to talk and the passing of the torch. A few years later Dad was called home to Heaven.

By this time, the herd seems irrelevant. I wondered if others had similar experiences with their fathers.

EVERYTHING IS IMPORTANT

N°! Everything cannot be important.

Really, it cannot. But if you listen to and observe most people, everything does seem important.

But if it all seems mission critical, how do we decide that which is truly most important?

What if we came face to face with a dire need to let go of some important things, what would we cut?

Trouble is we give up the will to effectively prioritize way too early in life, and pretend (for the rest of our lives) that some things are not more important than others. This supports the herd's belief that everything is important.

Think about it. If we actually believed some things were more important, we would have to behave differently. That would cause friction within our herd.

So I'm calling your herd's bluff. A classic put up or shut up moment.

Is everything important?

WE SIMPLY MUST HAVE A HEALTHY BALANCE IN THESE FIVE AREAS OF OUR LIFE

What is life's secret recipe for balance? Many think it is an either-or proposition. Work time versus personal time. I think it is the big five choices we talked about earlier:

1. **Mind** — mental responsibility, we think
2. **Body** — physical responsibility, we move
3. **Spirit** — emotional responsibility, we feel
4. **Money** — financial responsibility, we earn
5. **HQ** — personal administration, we dwell

Note: by dwell I mean we call someplace home, the place we sleep each night.

Popular opinion is that balance is about the amount of time spent between work and home.

Balance is not about time it is about energy. Energy expended (which takes time) to have five robust health accounts.

MID LIFE CELEBRATION'S MODEL

I thought long and hard about what is most important in life. Quite literally far more time than one might deem reasonable or acceptable.

As a professional speaker I have spoken to a million people so far and have grown up in, been trained to, recognized for, and entrusted with, preserving a world-renowned legacy of excellence. So I went to the classic foundation of all great teaching — strip a complex theory into the undeniable basics.

Some call it truth.

Finally convinced I had discovered the secret recipe, I drew it in less than a minute.

It is a deceptively simple model.

Mind – Body – Spirit – Money – HQ

WHEN YOU NEGLECT ONE OF THESE AREAS YOU WILL GET A WAKEUP CALL

MIND: Pollute your mental health — your attitude — and eventually the people you hang out with, the things you watch and listen to, the language and frame of mind you use, all these things will cause a major failure or breakdown in your attitude.

BODY: Avoid regular exercise, adequate rest, a balanced diet, annual examinations and your body will become so toxic, your life is in danger.

SPIRIT: Remain selfish, fail to serve, abstain from donating time, talent or treasure, forget the source of your infinite blessings, and you will find yourself lost in a deep, dark hole.

MONEY: Relax at work, go through the motions, spend more time thinking about leaving work than getting to work, hide from opportunities, responsibilities, projects, networking, and you will surely earn less than if you had earnestly applied yourself. But also remember that more salary is not necessarily better.

HQ: You are the CEO of your life. Your dwelling is your personal office where you handle the paperwork of life. Your level of competence for personal organization impacts every other area of your life.

WHEN YOU IGNORE THE WAKEUP CALLS, EVENTUALLY YOU WILL ARRIVE AT 'TOO LATE'

This is a lesson that once learned should last forever.

It is the lesson where if you do not get to the school bus stop on time you miss the bus.

The bus waits for no one.

Time waits for no one.

Midlife crisis is missing the bus for owning and delivering on our personal responsibilities.

Mid life celebration is that rare and glorious moment when the bus circles back to give us a second chance at life.

WHEN YOU NEGLECT ONE OF THESE AREAS TOO LONG, YOU WILL BE LESS EFFECTIVE IN THE OTHER AREAS

Take a traditional chair or table with multiple legs. If any one of the legs is longer or shorter than the others it obviously cannot be balanced. Life is like that too.

You cannot shortchange one leg without impacting the whole outcome.

You cannot overcompensate one leg without impacting the whole outcome.

You know this.

But do we fuss over it?

Do we work tirelessly to keep all five legs balanced?

If the vast majority of our herd lives without balance, does that give us permission to accept the same habits?

And does this conformity free us from guilt and obligation?

NO ONE SHOULD CARE MORE ABOUT YOUR PHYSICAL HEALTH THAN YOU

Who should care more about your health than you? (Not a trick question)

When you do not care about your health, well, what are you left with?

The last day you exercise is the healthiest you will ever be in your life. Think about that for a moment and let it sink in.

Your body is a temple housing everything that keeps you alive.

SAME WITH MENTAL, PHYSICAL, SPIRITUAL, FINANCIAL, AND HQ

Who should care more about your mental attitude, your physical health, your spiritual core, your career, and your home than you? No one.

When we become an adult, we become the person in charge. The CEO of You, Inc.

When we turned 18 we technically became an adult.

How much chief executive officer training did we receive?

Zero? Pretty close.

We spent 12 years in school learning math, science, history, reading, writing and all the other basics upon which society has deemed important in order to launch a child from home to being on their own.

What training did we receive for the personal responsibility imperative that focuses on mental, physical, spiritual, career, and home excellence?

We could call what we received a drop in the bucket.

Many of us deny this. Eventually, this decision comes around full circle and we pay the price. The CEO of You, Inc. files chapter 11.

MIND

We think with our mind.

Our mind nurtures our attitude, which determines whether we see things as opportunities or problems.

This nurturing is in our control.

This nurturing is our responsibility.

But alas, it is far easier to blend in than to take a stand. So we blend in.

Plus, nurturing is hard work, full of temptation to lighten up, to quit.

The people we hang out with, the books we read, the language we use, and the content of the media we watch heavily influence our attitude.

All of these are under our control.

And are our personal responsibilities.

No one else's.

BODY

Our body is our temple. It houses all the things that keep us alive. We should worship this marvelous miracle that surpasses all comprehension.

Being active is an innate trait for all young creatures. Being active is how we explore and learn about our environment and our place in it.

We know we must stay active as we get older and eat a balanced, sensible diet. But we often neglect sleep. We cannot neglect rest.

Rest is completely and overwhelmingly underrated.

All our efforts have a fundamental cause and effect that is our duty to manage well.

An object in motion tends to stay in motion.

Yet when we look around at any American community, most people are inactive and simply surviving.

All of these things are in our control.

And are our personal responsibilities.

We know this.

SPIRIT

Why would any of us not discern and embrace the source of our spirit — our emotions — and our ability to think rationally about our feelings?

Why? Because it is simply too easy to blend in and too hard to do what is right.

We possess as human beings an unshakable core belief, which is our mysterious desire to serve others. We are emotional, spiritual creatures.

Not embracing our core spirit and emotions is like getting a gift and never unwrapping it. Like saying thank you to the giver, but never knowing what is inside. Like being a confused pretender.

Humans have an irrepressible desire to help others less fortunate. Yet often our desire gets buried deep within the confines of going through the motions of the daily rat race.

And when we can eliminate our motive for personal gain we become a vessel for serving others.

Ironically we learn that in giving to others we actually receive more blessings than ever before. All of this is in our control, and is our responsibility.

It is no one else's.

MONEY

Every ant in the ant colony and every bee in the beehive makes a contribution. It is the same with humans. In modern society we are paid money in exchange for our contribution.

Developing our skills and broadening our experience all lead to higher earning potential. Our work life is our career.

We'll spend four or five decades doing this.

Remember that more money doesn't necessarily mean a better situation. And be careful what you wish for — you just might get it.

Also, please do not complain if you did not try hard enough.

How we apply ourselves and manage the motives behind our goals and behave moving forward, is within our control.

And our career is our personal responsibility.

It belongs to no one else.

HQ

HQ is the paperwork of life.

And the paperwork of life will be our responsibility until we die.

Being organized is better than not being organized. Everything works more smoothly when we are decently organized. We are not aiming for being perfectly organized. Strive for perfection but settle for excellence.

Being decently organized positively impacts our other four big life choices.

Being disorganized negatively impacts our other four big life choices: mind, body, spirit, and money (work).

We cannot tolerate disorganization. Ever. Because life will strenuously challenge us when we least expect it.

What we accept by default becomes our standard and we may slowly become blinded to and overwhelmed by the mountain of administrative challenges we have unintentionally created.

We should be careful, thoughtful, and considerate about any mess we leave behind for someone else to worry about.

RECOMMIT

10 QUESTIONS
TO CONSIDER — MIND:

1. My thoughts are clear, optimistic, and admirable?
2. What I read is moral, diverse, and encouraging?
3. I actively and enthusiastically learn and teach?
4. I see opportunity where others see problems?
5. My priorities are rock solid and crystal clear?
6. What I watch and listen to in the media is positive?
7. I associate with positive, admirable people?
8. I am able to stay positive during crisis or tragedy?
9. I have control over my language?
10. I am one of the most positive people I know?

10 QUESTIONS
TO CONSIDER — BODY:

1. I always know how much I weigh?
2. I know my cholesterol levels?
3. I check my blood pressure at least monthly?
4. I know my BMI (body mass index)?
5. I know my triglyceride levels?
6. I know my resting heart rate?
7. I exercise regularly?
8. My eating portions, choices, and quality are good?
9. I know my health goals?
10. My health beliefs and habits are practiced daily?

10 QUESTIONS
TO CONSIDER — SPIRIT:

1. I know the meaning of life?
2. I constantly live with gratitude?
3. I constantly live with compassion?
4. I constantly live with forgiveness?
5. I constantly live with joy?
6. I accept fear as merely attachment to things?
7. I know what I can control and what I cannot?
8. I start every morning on my knees?
9. I am here to serve and not to be served?
10. I live without regret and with humble anticipation?

10 QUESTIONS TO CONSIDER — MONEY:

1. I spend less than I earn?
2. I have positive net worth (assets minus liabilities)?
3. I have access to a CPA and an Attorney if needed?
4. I have a will?
5. My self-image is not tied to my possessions?
6. I donate financially to charity?
7. I have at least one passive income source?
8. I have diversified my investments and assets?
9. I have a decent (at least 90 days) rainy day fund?
10. I know my retirement date and plan afterwards?

10 QUESTIONS
TO CONSIDER — HQ:

1. I consider myself organized?
2. I know the pros and cons of personal organization?
3. I model the most organized person I know?
4. I learn from the most disorganized person I know?
5. I have backup plans for my backup plans?
6. I admit being organized can feel overwhelming?
7. I picture worse case scenario if I do not keep up?
8. I have my most important documents protected?
9. I use technology to easily change and update things?
10. I mastered a password system for my accounts?

RECOMMIT

Recommit is defined as: Pledge or bind to a certain course. In this case, recommitting to a different course than the one we have followed our entire life.

We must pledge and bind ourselves to set a new course.

This is our personal responsibility, and no one else's.

FEAR

The challenge with truly and fully committing is that it is such a radical departure from our old lifestyle that the odds of us succeeding are slim. And we know this.

Keep in mind slim does not imply that it is impossible. This is great news!

But keep in mind that slim elicits fear in most people — especially the fear of pain in the transition to going way out of our comfort zone.

Not to mention the fear of failing late in the game of life and losing everything.

In your journey you have come to realize that taking risks is risky and so is playing it safe. Playing it safe will lead to additional disappointment in the future. You know this.

Taking a few small risks to **reprioritize** and **recommit** will change you and change everything about you moving forward.

Fear is our attachment to things such as comfort. Letting go of our comfort is similar to starting over.

But think of yourself as an 18 year old with 20, 30 or even 40 years experience.

IT IS TOO MUCH WORK

So, we have worked our whole life to reach a certain status, comfort level, and standard of living.

Now we are proposing to discount our entire life's work? To become someone other than who we spent our lives becoming?

Are we insane?

It is too much effort, too much risk, too late in the game. Right?

Like we have heard before, taking risks is risky. So is playing it safe.

Go! We must go.

It is our personal responsibility.

No one else will do this for us.

Ever.

I CANNOT DO IT

I cannot do it and not only that, I will not.

This is okay to say a few times.

Saying it humanizes our herd mentality.

But fairly quickly we realize we need to get over it.

Seriously.

Please know you are not alone in wanting to break free from the herd.

Those of us who have broken free and escaped for good, at one time just like you are experiencing now, quietly and desperately longed to be more vibrant, more alive, and more intentional.

But the herd is mean and makes fun of those trying to break away, trying to make us feel guilty in wanting to leave.

But those who escaped took their personal responsibility to a higher level.

Recommit to your escape? How can you not?

WHY DID YOU DECIDE
TO DO THIS?

With the echo of I cannot do this ringing in your ear there is good news.

And the reason there is good news is because of that mantra that *we own our life and are personally responsible for all of it*.

This has you **rethinking**. This is good.

Rethinking your priorities.

And then **reprioritizing** your life in a way that is so much healthier than the way you have been living.

And you know this will require change and change requires commitment.

But our historical track record is fairly dismal.

The good news is you **recommit** anyway. Why?

Because there is a deep down, unexplainable, intuitive, burning fire inside you to achieve the real, true goal: Service to others. And so you press on.

By now you fully comprehend in a way that has never resonated so strongly, that your life is not a dress rehearsal.

WHAT AM I GETTING BY STAYING THIS WAY?

This is one of those questions that will easily tip the scale so that we **do** go against the odds.

What am I getting by not changing?

We know there is something bigger, more comfortable, more rewarding, more invigorating, more important than we have ever done before.

And we want all of it. And we deserve all of it.

We actually, at the end of our careful **rethinking**, see it as a no-brainer to **reprioritize** and **recommit**.

DO IT FOR SOMEONE MORE IMPORTANT

Do it for someone else. This is the yeast in life's recipe for success, the sweet aroma of peace and contentment.

Selfish goals no longer satisfy us and the only way our new hunger can be fed is with selfless goals. And the greatest motivator of all is to identify someone more important than you.

When we are stuck in disbelief and doubt we are actually very close to the truth.

The truth is we are not here to be served.

Time has a patient plan of ever so slowly teaching us this in a way that finally sinks in deeply enough for change to begin.

This is that time.

You know this.

How cool is it to finally admit?

That we are here to serve and not to be served.

And so we slowly and somewhat reluctantly take our place at the end of the line.

YOUR DECISIONS ARE INFLUENCING OTHERS

Passion is contagious. Unfortunately, passion does not always work for the greater good. Remember Hitler?

But when passion is lit for the greater good, there is no force on Earth that can hold back the passion to do good work.

The second most contagious thing in the world is the lack of enthusiasm.

The first is of course, the opposite — being so full of enthusiasm, that you infect others without even trying.

Let your newly found enthusiasm be the most contagious thing in the world. Yet remain humble enough to not annoy or turn off others.

Your decision has ripple effects. The greater your passion and commitment, the larger your ripples.

How cool is that?

It is okay to high five yourself right now if you want.

ARE YOU AN EXAMPLE
OR A WARNING?

We must find our own trigger that centers us, grounds us, and reminds us. Something that the very moment we think of it, we are immediately refocused on the sheer importance of what must be done and why.

When someone important in our life thinks of the way we have lived, how do we think they will answer this question, the one we also silently ask ourselves?

Am I an example or a warning?

ACT! THE CHANGE HAS TO BE FOR SOMEONE ELSE

When we do things to satisfy ourselves and we fail, we are the only ones we let down.

Oddly we can live with our own guilt because unfortunately, we have become experts at rationalizing that this is okay.

Besides, everyone else in our herd rationalizes it this way too.

When we do things for someone more important than ourselves and we fail, the consequences are much more significant.

If we really care, our desire should be so intense at succeeding that our resolve to never quit becomes indomitable.

Our acts of love, of courage, and of purpose will inspire those following us to do the same when they are faced later in their lives with the devil's temptation to quit.

PERSEVERE

Persevere is perhaps one of the most underrated words in history.

It is also an uncommon characteristic within our herd.

Our length of perseverance to a large extent, determines our success or failure.

The only way to *persevere* is to not quit. Ever.

CAN YOU OUTLAST THE FEAR?

Fear is the key reason perseverance might not become our success factor.

Indecision feeds fear, sustains fear, and actually enlarges fear's reach.

Do not be afraid of going slowly. Be only afraid of standing still.

And remember fear is attachment. Do not be attached to personal gain.

The desire for personal gain poisons our soul.

History demonstrates this with a remarkably simple observation: no one on their deathbed wishes they would have spent more time at the office.

MAKE INCREMENTAL PROGRESS

We live one day at a time.
No really, we do.

Sounds cliché, but we simply cannot live in tomorrow and we cannot live in yesterday.

Today if we take only one step forward, it is one step closer to where we are going.

We can always take more than one step each day. In fact there is no limit to the number.

But if we take no step forward then, indeed, no step forward has been taken.

You do the math if this bleeds into the next day, and the next and the next.

BECOME FRIENDS WITH FEAR

Fear is a survival instinct. It's one of the greatest gifts we are given as humans. The ability to sense danger and take flight or fight.

What we can distill from fear is the reality that worrying about daily survival (getting eaten) in a civilized world is no longer an issue.

Why we still allow fear to paralyze us is a mystery. What if we confronted fear and simply saw it as relentless attempts by the devil to distract us?

Do what you fear and the death of that fear will come.

Detach yourself from the fear of dying?

Yes.

Replace it with the joyful blessing of being alive today.

Find joy in your gratitude, your compassion, and your forgiveness.

Find your peace and contentment in knowing death is undeniably the third most magnificent day in our lives.

How? It is finally the day we can rejoice in getting to travel to our next stage in life. Eternal life.

THE SECOND BEGINNING
(MOVING ON FROM HERE)

REALIZE THE INVESTMENT

When we invest in changing our comfort zone and achieve little victories we begin to see a broader, brighter horizon.

When we continually practice doing what is uncomfortable, we gradually become more successful.

We get better at the things we repeatedly do.

The great jugglers of the world make it look easy. How? They made a bigger investment in time, energy, and opportunity than the good jugglers.

It is the same in any endeavor.

We know this.

Realize that your investment is your closest ally in overcoming your previous habits.

And if we want to change, the responsibility falls on us.

No one else is responsible for our change.

Ever.

FIND A NEW HERD

Birds of a feather flock together. Look around. Do the people, attitudes, goals, dreams, effort, hope, sacrifice — do the people in your herd inspire you to do great things to serve others more selflessly?

If your answer is no but you wish it were yes, you must find a new herd.

Period.

You know this.

This is truth.

It is your responsibility.

It is no one else's.

TO MAKE ROOM FOR SOMETHING NEW GET RID OF SOMETHING OLD

A wise boss long ago told me that in order to create something new, something else had to be destroyed.

If you want paper you must destroy the tree.

If you want more time to _____, you must stop (destroy) _____.

Destroy one habit in exchange for another habit.

There is no other way and thinking there is another option is as absurd as saying you can add extra hours to your day.

Once again Mid Life Celebration's mantra is here to refocus exactly what we need to do:

Rethink.

Reprioritize.

Recommit.

FORGIVE

Perhaps no other action we can do yields results with a higher degree of return on investment.

What forgiveness does for our spirit (our soul) is what food does for our appetite and what water does for our thirst.

We cannot fathom going very long without eating and drinking. What if we felt that way about forgiveness?

So right here right now, practice.

Forgive yourself for your midlife crisis.

Pause.

I can wait.

No really. I can wait.

Okay, thank you for forgiving yourself. That was the first of perhaps 1,000+ gracious self-forgiving moments.

Pat yourself on the back.

And smile.

AFFIRM WHAT YOU DESERVE

I am not worthy. We hear this echoing in our ears.

Intellectually, physically, emotionally, professionally, and at home, we want it all. But we are not worthy. Only the richest, smartest, healthiest, most centered people get great rewards.

Really?

Do you really believe this deep down in your soul?

Wealth is way more than money. You know this. And you know that every human is worthy and deserving.

Repeat. Every human is worthy and deserving.

You are worthy and deserving.

Pause.

Personal forgiveness opportunity number two: forgive yourself for thinking you had to meet a certain criteria to be worthy. Okay, good. Thank you.

We must stop acting like we are ignorant. We are not.

Go. You deserve it. And keep smiling.

SET GOALS

Not setting goals is like commanding a ship without a rudder. You know this.

Goals can be rewritten, tossed aside, dusted off. You have a variety of options. Goals can be anything you want.

And please do not sell yourself short. Reach. Stretch. Change. Have fun. Be excited. And cry if you have to.

And here is a personal challenge. Set a goal you can achieve within 72 hours after finishing this book.

Why? Because your herd is expecting you back any day now.

And after three days humans have a funny habit of going back to the same path simply because it is easier. We like easy.

You know this too. No one else will do it for you.

Start small.

Rethink. Reprioritize. Recommit.

REMEMBER LIFE HAS FIVE BIG CHOICES

So having only one goal to accomplish in the next 72 hours is the beginning. You are going to feel so good about getting one in your win column.

Setting and achieving this easy win gives you the taste of victory you deserve and the reassurance that going slowly in the beginning is perfectly acceptable. One day at a time. Okay?

In fact, going slow is recommended.

Here is your one note of caution: the process cannot be circumvented. **Rethink** is first, then **reprioritize**, and then you **recommit**.

You will eventually (and fairly quickly, say a month or so) want goals in all five areas of your life. And you will gradually ramp up to living with all five areas front and center, every single day, for the rest of your life.

Mind. Body. Spirit. Money. HQ

A reminder that a great place for you to start is to return to the section in this book with the 10 questions from each life choice. Remember those questions?

Mind. Body. Spirit. Money. HQ

How cool is that?

INVEST IN YOUR OWN TRUTH

One of the most difficult things for us to do is to learn to listen to and trust our own voice.

We become so conditioned to thinking we need to get approval before we think a decision is correct.

When we start making decisions without asking or waiting for approval, we move into a place away from the herd. And we move from being unintentionally irresponsible to being intentionally responsible.

We have all been given an instinct and gut feelings for a reason. You know this.

Not discovering our own voice and following it is one of life's greatest challenges and biggest tragedies.

The **second most magnificent day in your life** is figuring out why you were born.

Now you know this. And now you are so much closer to understanding why you were born.

You have been baptized with the challenge of personal responsibility: to **rethink**, **reprioritize**, and **recommit**.

EPILOGUE

A crisis as we have learned, is when we get to a significant milestone in our life, one in which we dreamt of and worked hard to achieve, only to discover it wasn't what we really wanted after all.

The beauty in our life is that wake up calls are really our Creator's gift to us to **Rethink, Reprioritize** and **Recommit**.

A year from now you will wish you had begun today.

Or if you start within 72 hours, one year from now you will be enjoying a heightened level of peace and contentment.

And whether you become an example or a warning will be the key driver for everything you do. And you will be conscious of this all day, everyday.

In the end it all comes down to personal responsibility.

And we all know it.

Be well and remain amazed.

Go.

DO SOMETHING GREAT

One final thought please.

I heard a story about President Abraham Lincoln's chief aid, a church-going man, and convinced the new Pastor at his church was the greatest Pastor he had ever heard, he invited President Lincoln to hear this Pastor speak.

After the sermon, the aid chased President Lincoln down and asked, President Lincoln, well, do you think he is the greatest Pastor you have ever heard?

To which Lincoln replied, No! Your Pastor shared great insight, but he did not ask any of us to do something great.

So dear reader, please, go do something great.

THE CHALLENGE

Do something great. Mend an important relationship before it is too late. Help find a cure for an incurable disease, or do something in between.

Go. Get started within 72 hours. Go. Now.

It is your personal responsibility.

It is no one else's.

You know this.

HOPE

The world is full of stories whereby ordinary people – people like you and me — decided to do something great and spent the rest of their lives not resting until they knew, with all the peace and contentment the world had to offer, that they had done their very best to serve others and do what they could to help make the world a better place.

A COMMUNITY

There is strength in numbers. Momentum is started by one person and kept alive and built stronger by a community. You are that community. You must be that community.

And in the end, the people that you love will watch you, remember your example and say, I hope someday I can be like that.

Go! Do something great!

The end.

(Or maybe just the beginning)

ACKNOWLEDGEMENTS

There are too many people to list individually. If you and I are family, friends, have worked together, or we have interacted somewhere in the world, my deepest gratitude to you for helping to positively influence and graciously shape life on our planet.

AUTHOR BIO

Like many others, jeff noel is simply a servant, husband, dad, son, brother, uncle, cousin, nephew, coworker, neighbor, volunteer, and sinner; perfectly imperfect.

He is deeply grateful for the blessing to be able to love and be loved, to forgive, to experience joy, and to run, write, and teach.

In jeff's wildest dreams, he visualizes personal responsibility for life's five big choices occupying sacred space in our educational system, from Pre-K through college.

www.MidLifeCelebration.com

jeff.noel@me.com

CPSIA information can be obtained at www.ICGtesting.com
Printed in the USA
BVOW08s1553150114

341958BV00001B/40/P